I0483929

JELLYFISH

JAY SNODGRASS

2 0 1 5

©2015 JAY SNODGRASS
Hysterical Books
Tallahassee, FL Thomasville, GA
ISBN 978-1508960751

for Kristine

*

This lamp made from the
oil of your experience
flickers the black, leaps
so lightly the grief lifts your hair
yet you smile from the depths of lead
whispers cast in rough ingots
your hair is brown like winter grass.

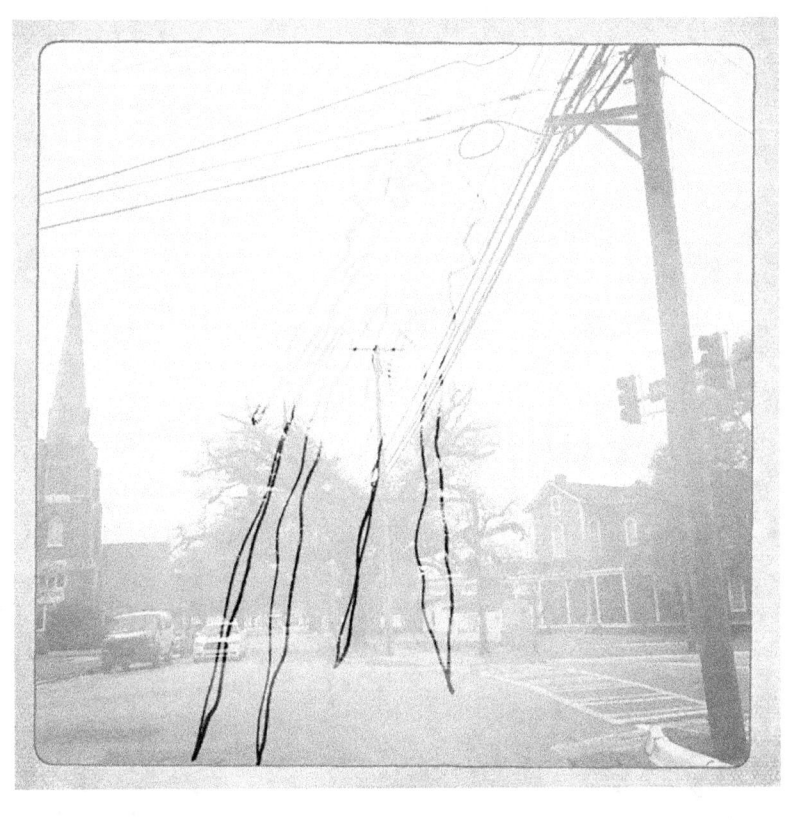

✳

Dandelion trace
yellow split road through dynamited granite
fast food restaurants on the hinge
of night
creak with secret commerce

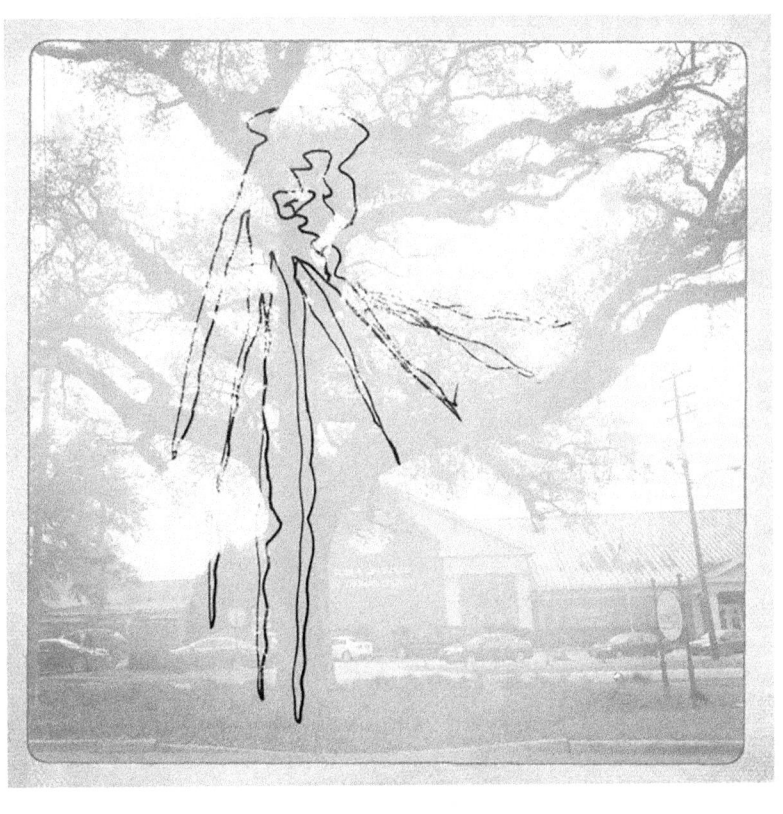

✶

Alive in the mirror, unshaven,
trying to choose correctly
from a whole countertop of sadness.

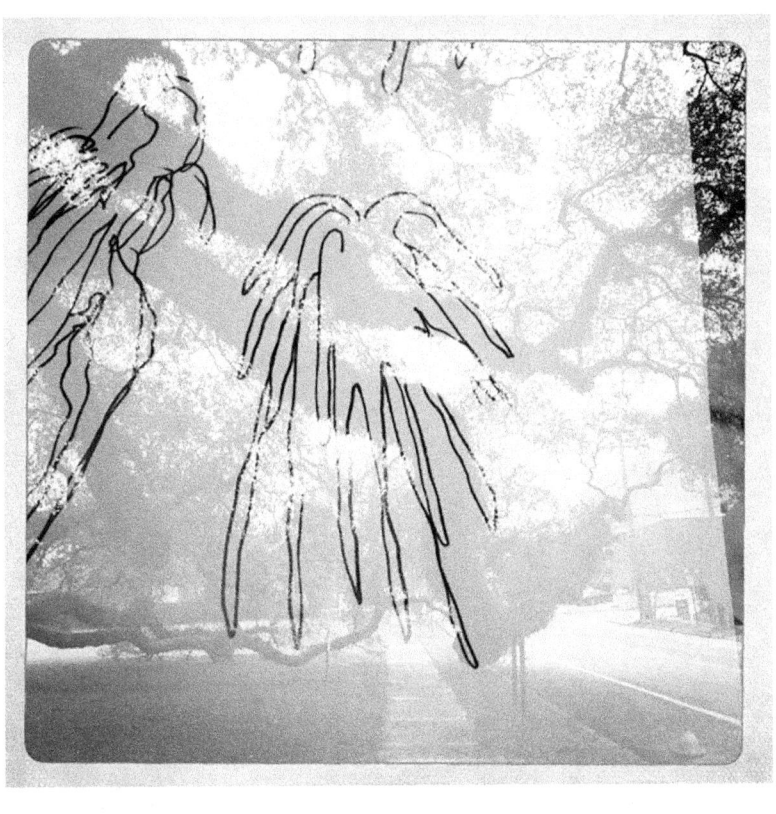

✽

I have set out your urn
among the other ingredients,
raw dust of seaside cliffs,
nourishment of air and dream.

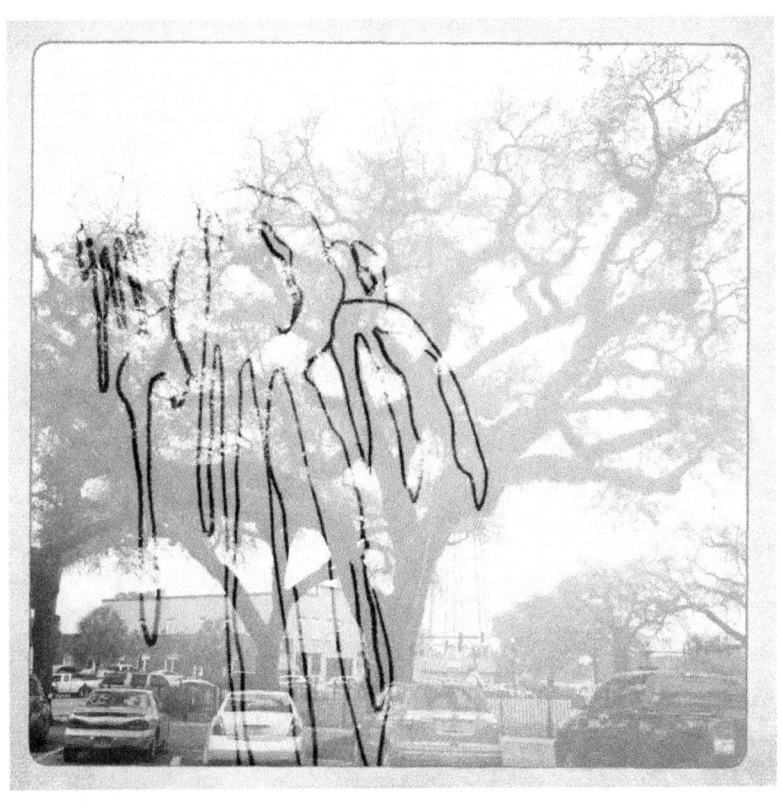

*

I am costumed to draw the eye
of the marksman, hidden in the obvious
landscape. Leaves assembled
to defend me.

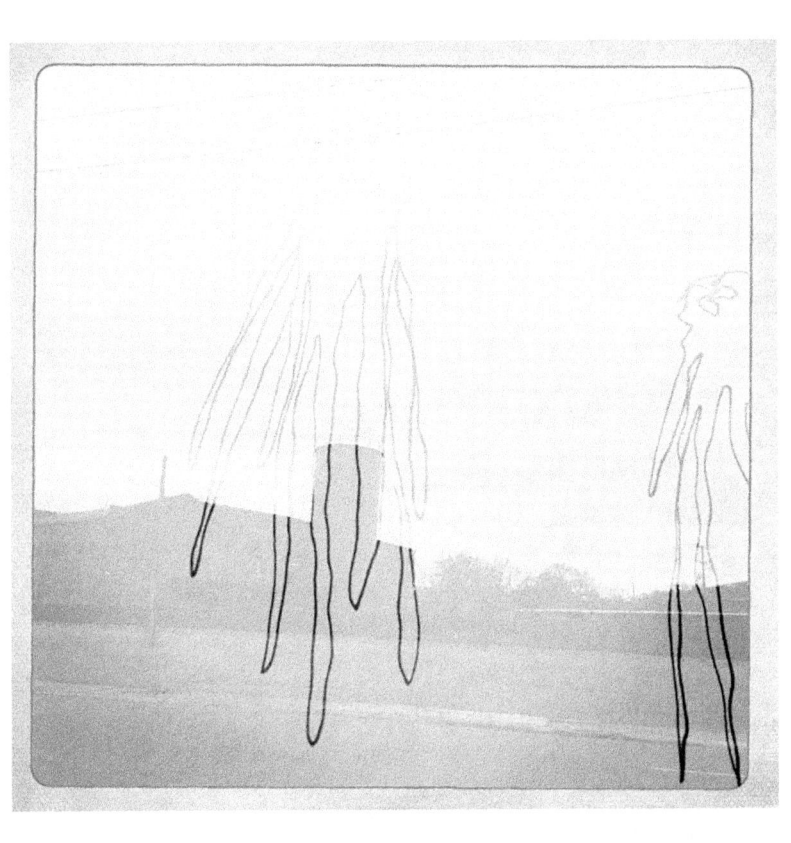

✻

In the midst of my prayers
the connection timed out,
all data was lost.

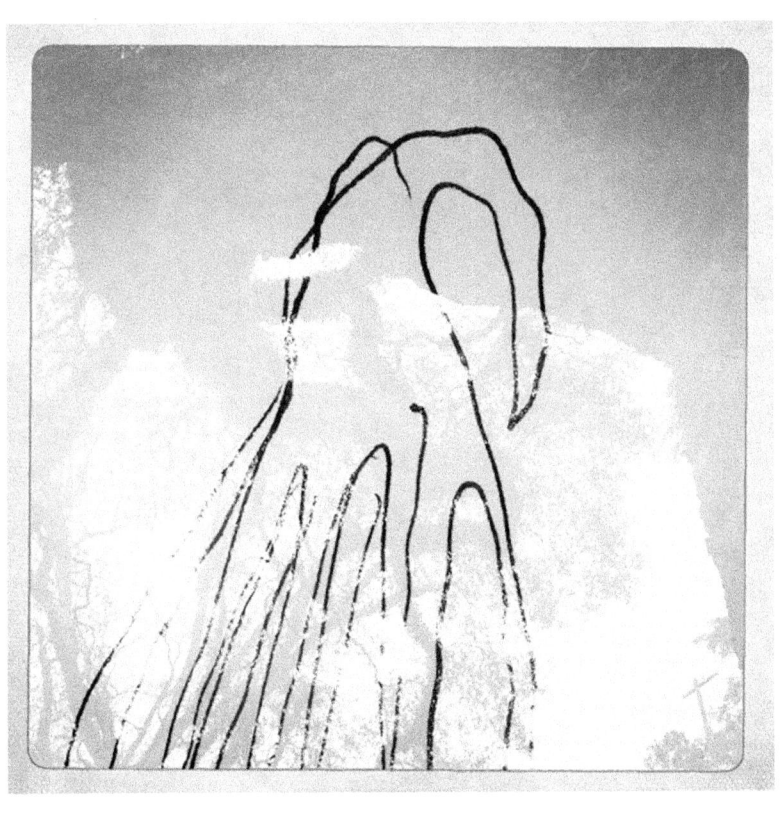

✲

I've sopped the sunset of your smile
with a kerchief. Silks
expressed by the hungriest worm.

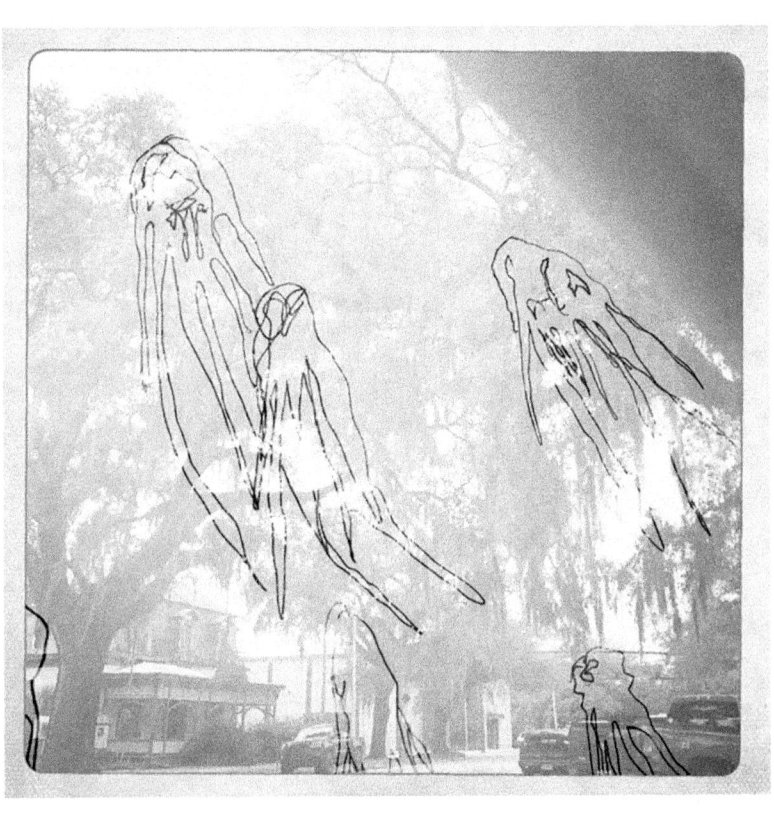

✿

I have rolled for fun and oblivion
the star-cut die, the peddler's hand,
the chance to catch a cup with air.

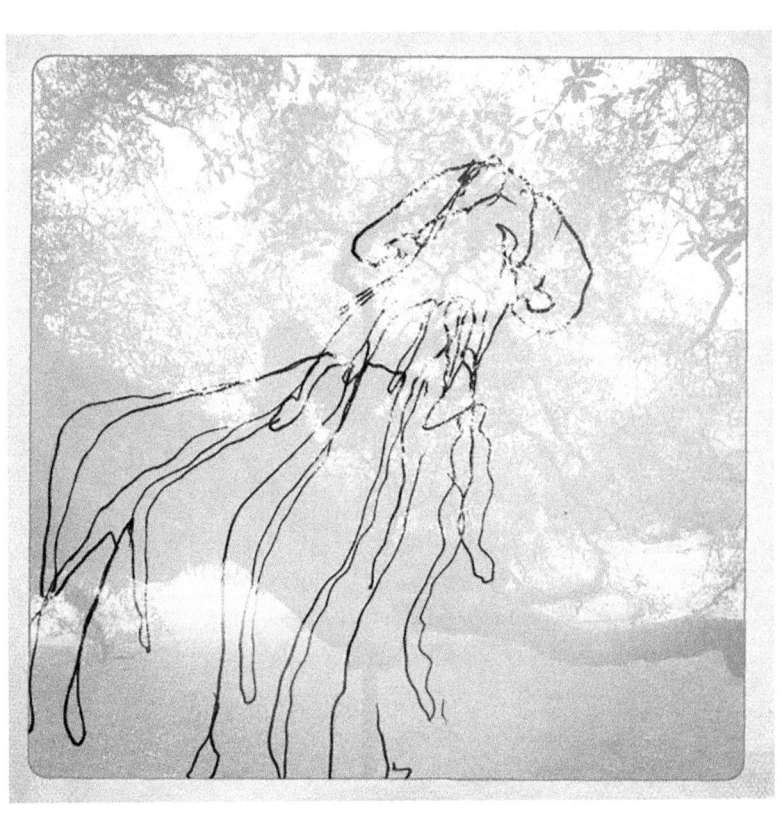

*

In the hotel room the sun never
goes down. We call the desk clerk
who sends a boy to remove the sun
and hides its abundance behind
a closet door where it molds bedside the pool
of infinites.

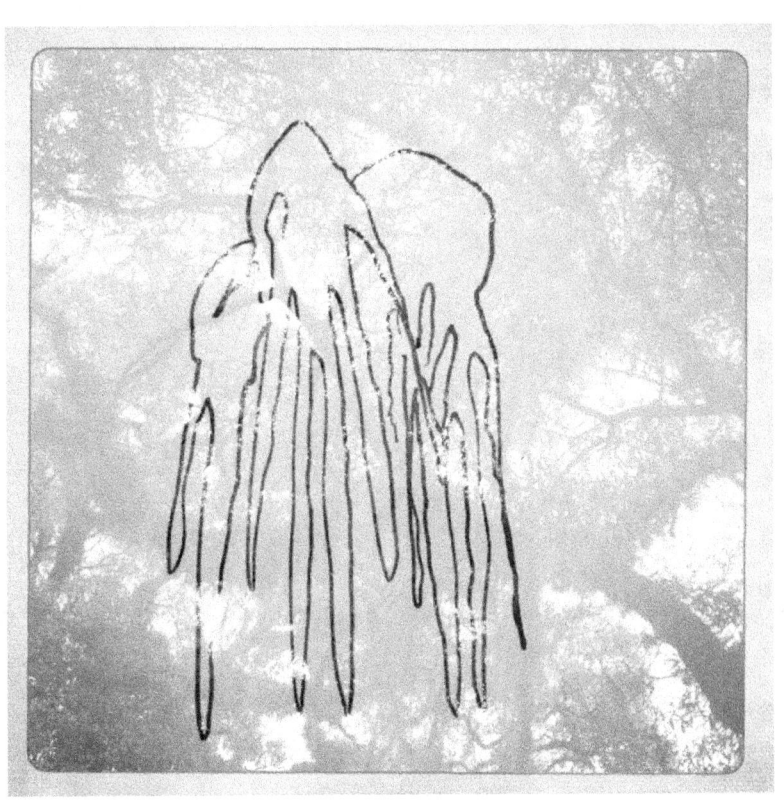

*

Speak you beheader of flowers,
bean composer,
leaf strummer. Speak to the window
as you pare the bell peppers.
Carve your name with teeth.

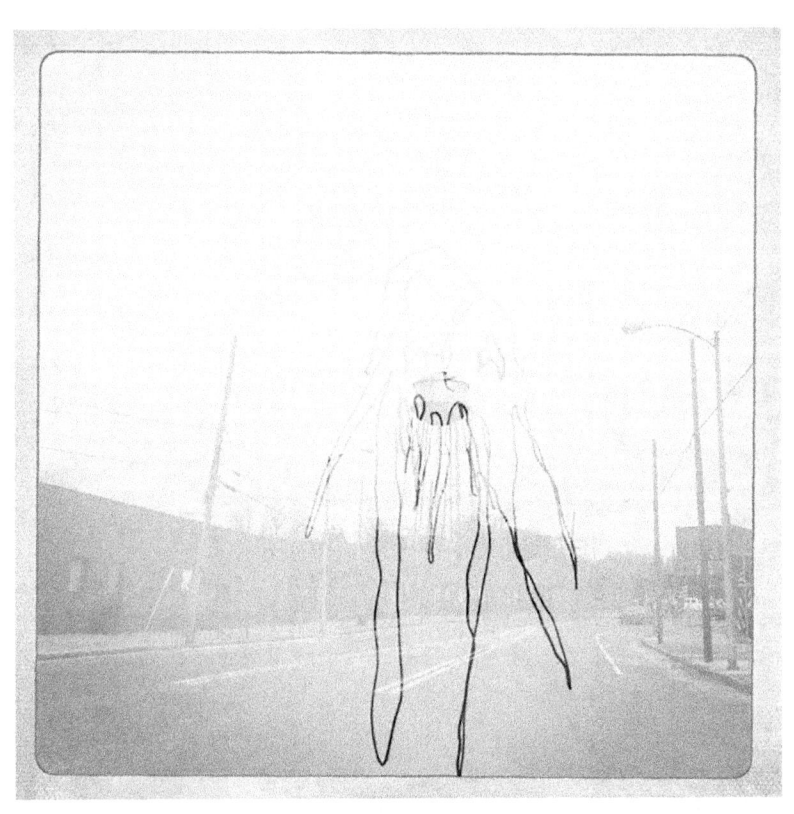

*

One wears the movements of my hand,
the shimmer of my touch,
a vanity I shed. Who finds it
can only believe they are inoculated against
all the waves of air in a year, the crenellation
of goodbyes, the carless grooves in beach sand
I pretended to be distracted by until I fall
apart, gesture by gesture. And he finds me.

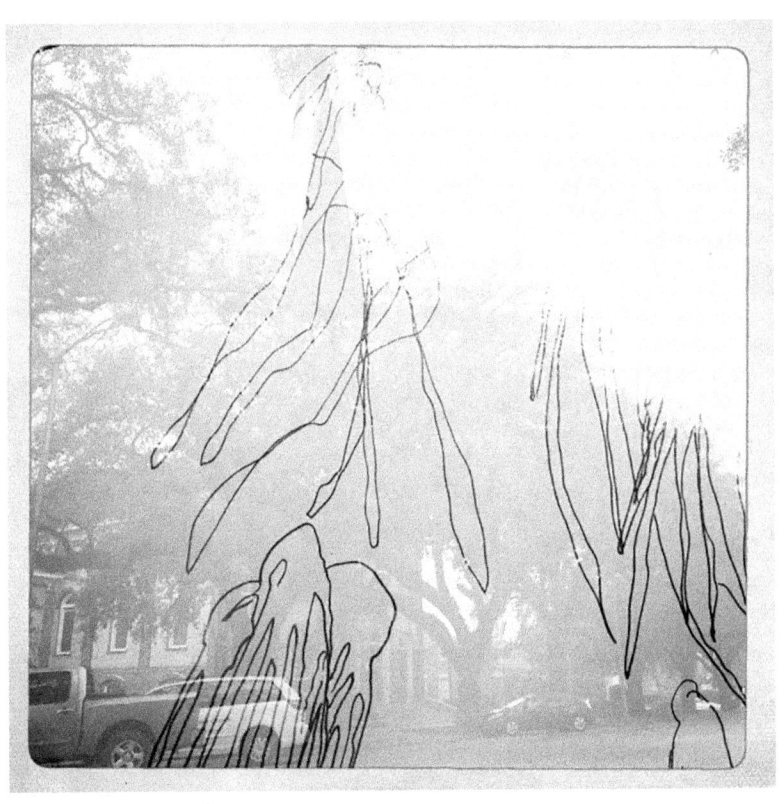

*

The one who wins opens his mouth
(the door) to speak the numbers.
Red-ball, distant sun becoming giant
in wonder, spreading like the mouth
around a word before it dissolves.
Tulips wilt, in the sun, bowing their heads.

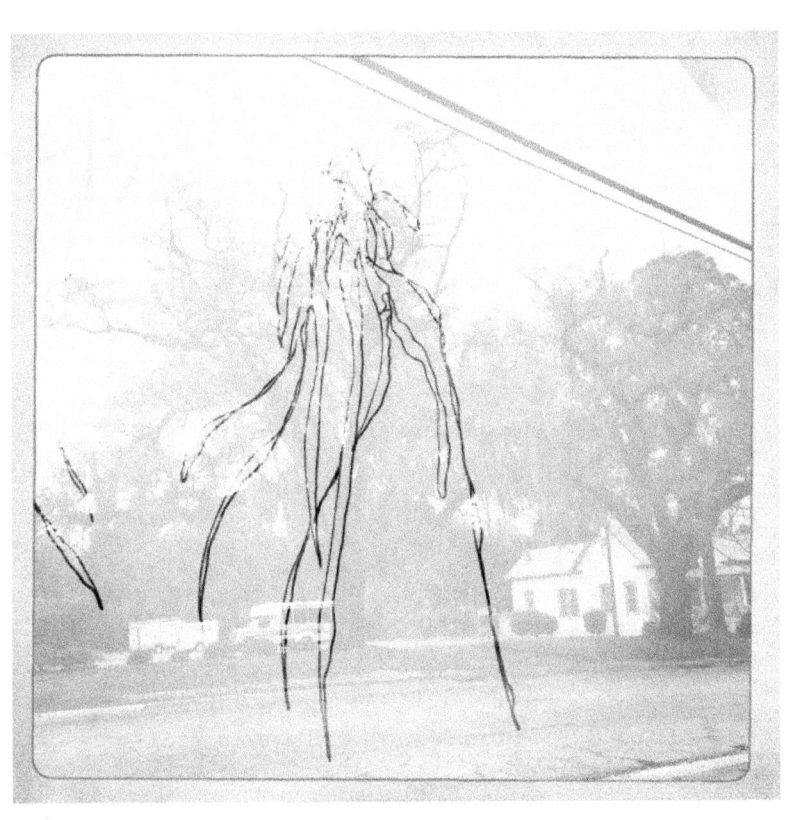

✳

Bone embedded in the callous,
bone inside the bone, buried
but alive, bone supporting bone,
coffin bone, the memory of your kiss
eroding me.

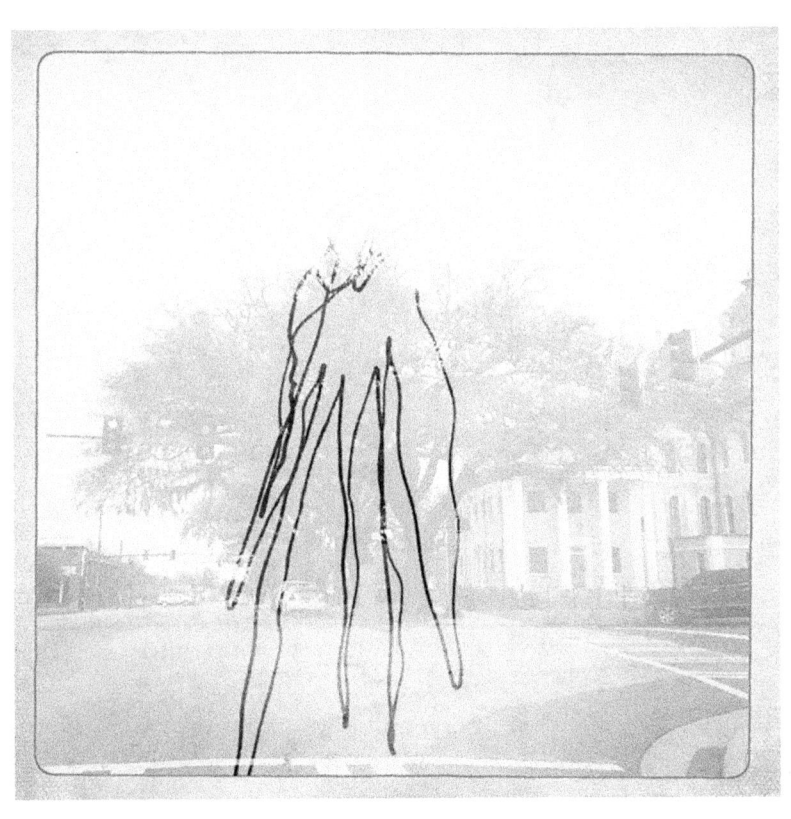

✻

Frozen baby birds sleep through winter
like spies on a stakeout. They are silent
as their dry eyes photograph my drug use
or my singing. Whatever it is, I lament.

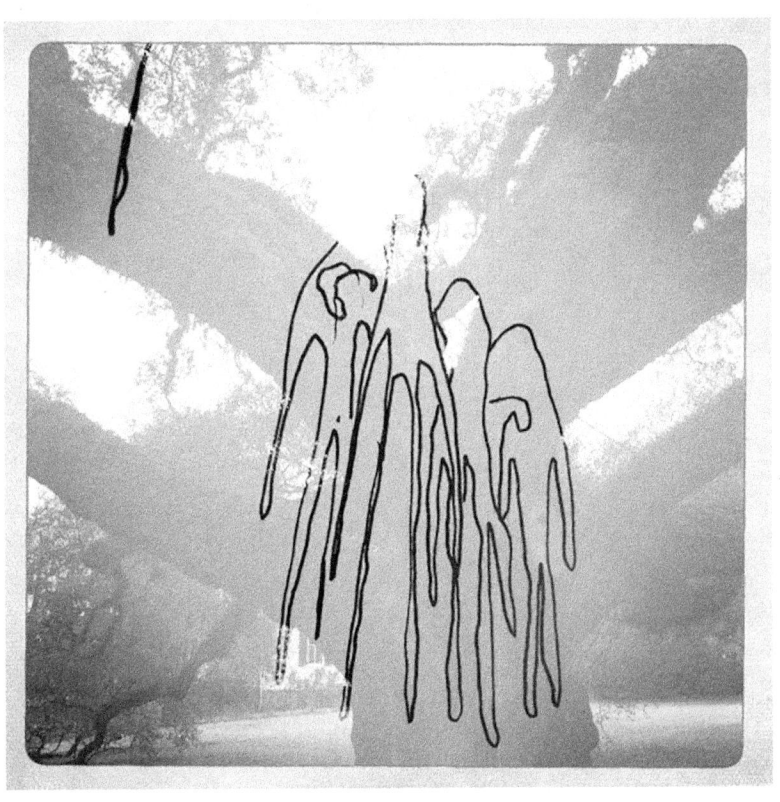

*

I wave to you, astronaut, through the galaxies,
wave away the distance. Light laps the darkness.

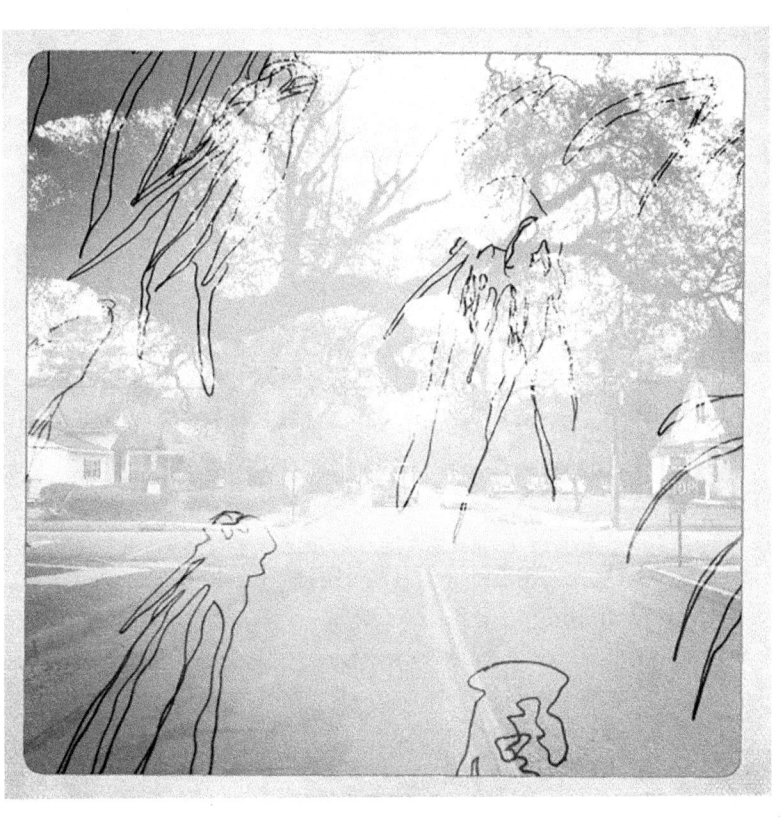

*

I share a dream with you through the Sunday Paper,
wrinkling its ink, alerting,
the table of forest leaves moved by wind.
Something is coming to us, an army in urgent uniforms,
a catastrophe of commerce, spilling
inserts across a desert floor.

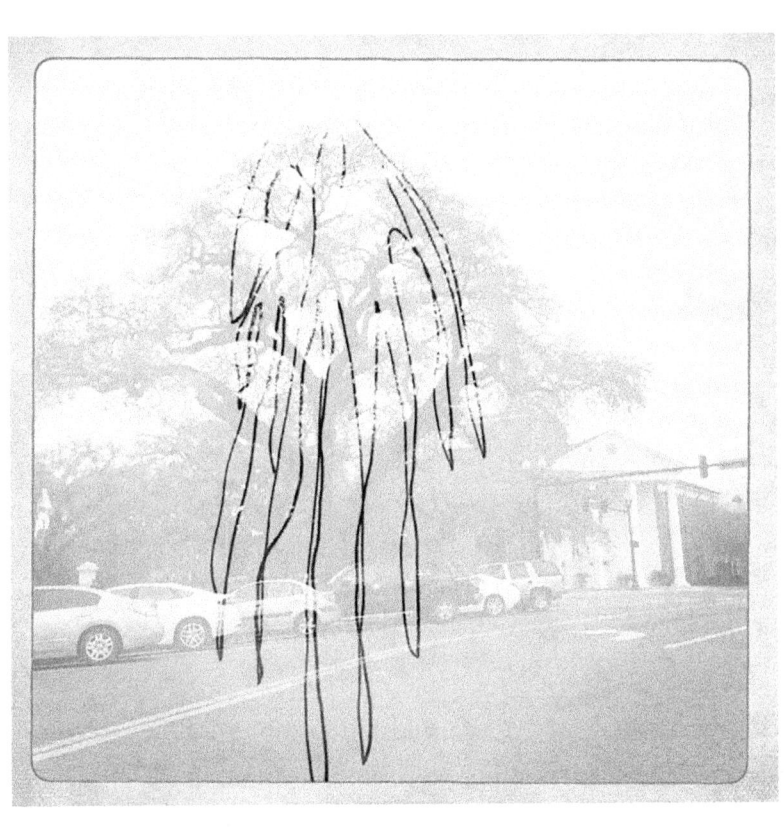

✳

It's time you knew, distemper and celery,
a sale on imports, your nerves, severe.
The wiring is bad. Sometimes
in the rain, it effervesces,
a sweet rainbow in my cup of disease.

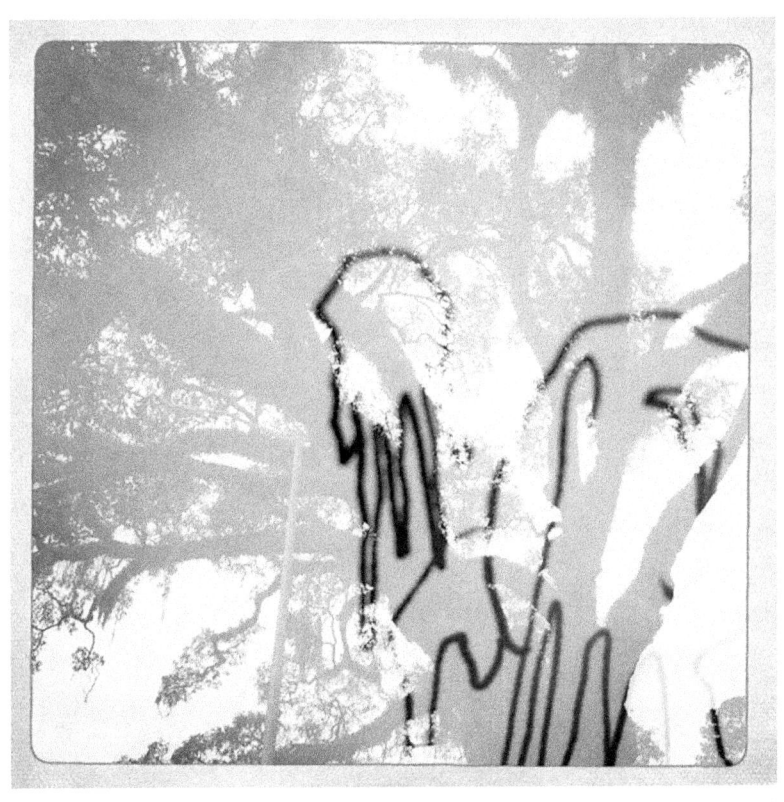

✫

Pass the nickel, palms to palms
for entry to the secret backrooms
where whiskey and milk are like daybreak.

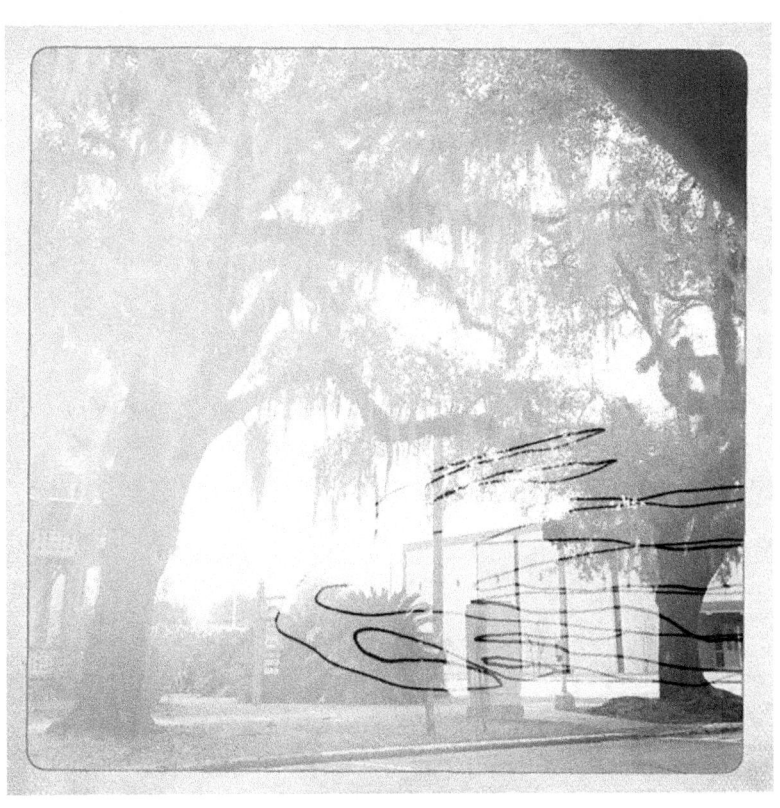

*

Hail and March, the blustery baron
sets aside his monocle, prepares to declare
last measures and forgiveness,
says dog stripes are agreeable
waves the kerchief of approval
and smoke fills the forest to announce.

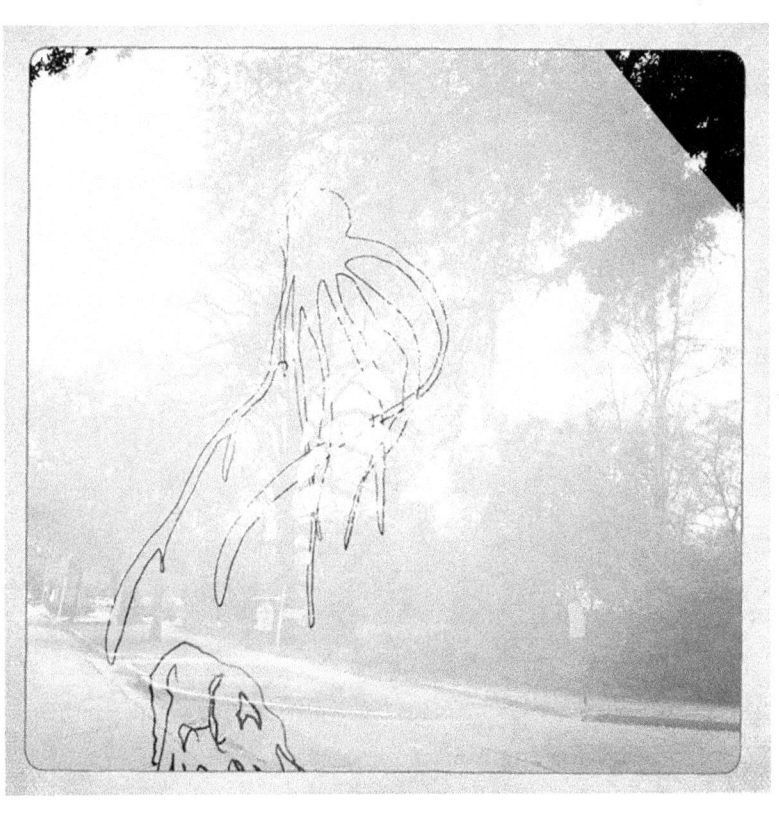

✼

The motivating shadow arrives
to sleep on your couch. Can you say no?
The motivating shadow comments on the dirty dishes.
The motivating shadow becomes the mother
inspecting your overlooked elements,
finds you wanting.

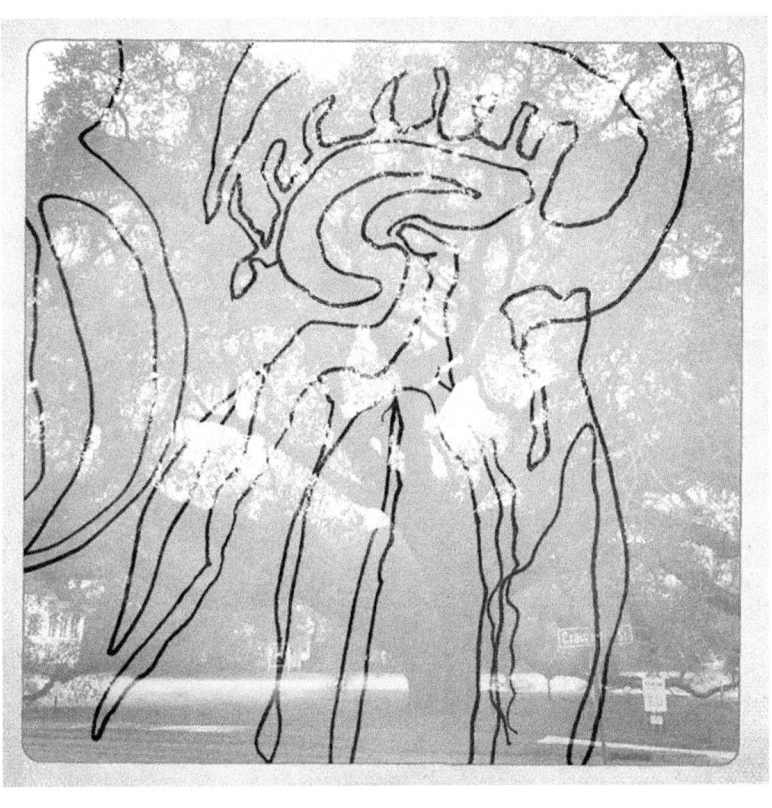

✣

The long gowns, eternal town,
the temples and occlusion, look.

Night paid me in sheckles,
glittering exchange like proverbs.

What you can't see absorbs
what you can.

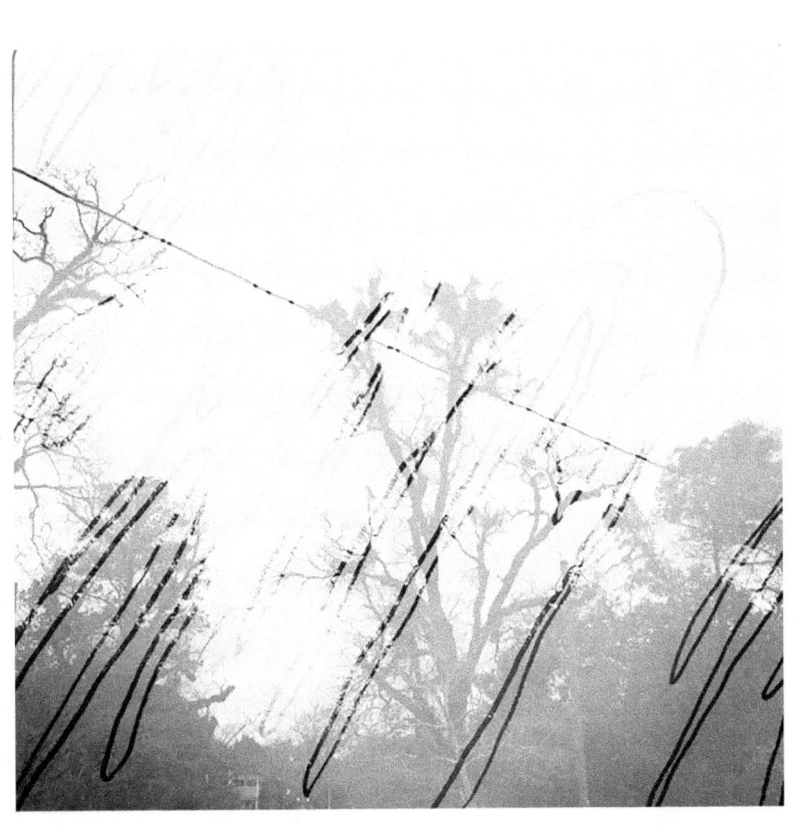

*

The séance of moonlight on the ocean
like a reading of stone.
The moon is lashed to the boom
over the sea like a sail,
traveler and prisoner.

✲

Sometimes you can find yourself
curiously floating in a sea
of eyes.

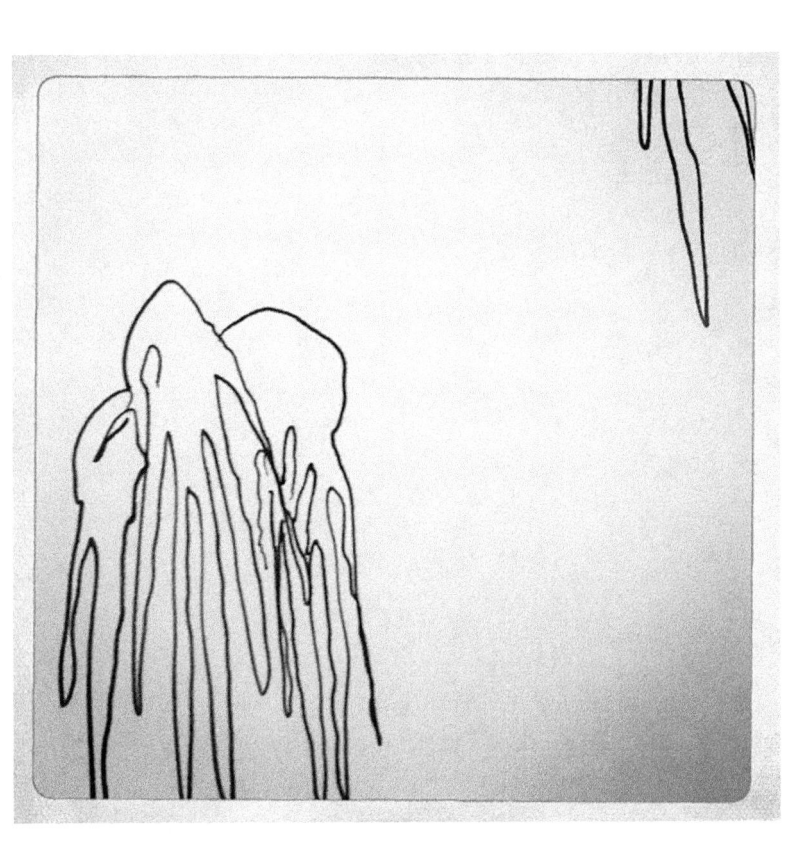

Made for Artist's Residency
Thomasville Center for the Arts
Thomasville, Georgia.

JELLYFISH

JAY SNODGRASS

2015

www.ingramcontent.com/pod-product-compliance
Lightning Source LLC
Chambersburg PA
CBHW070515210526
45168CB00021B/2105